Fit for the Kingdom

A SPIRITUAL FITNESS DEVOTIONAL

GABRIELLE JACKSON

Cover Illustration Copyright © 2015 by Gabrielle Jackson
Cover design by Studio 5 Agency
Publishing and Editing by Keen Vision Publishing
Author photograph by Jeremy Marc Anthony McBean

ISBN: (978-0692596937)

KEEN VISION PUBLISHING

Acknowledgements

To my beautiful and supportive mother, Cassandra Jackson, thank you for always being in my corner and on my team. I love you. To my amazing family, thank you just simply doesn't do justice to my appreciation for your unwavering support throughout this process. I love you all dearly. Special thanks to my All Nations Christian Center Church family, my Pastor, and friends for continuously pouring into me and helping me to achieve my lifelong goal of becoming an author.

Fit for the Kingdom is a fitness spiritual devotional. The scriptures used in this devotional are not property of the author or publishing company. Neither claim scriptures as creative property. Scriptures are used to support readers as they connect life application to the word of God.

About the Author

"It would be a shame to work so hard to be fit for the world, and be unfit for the King." This quote outlines Gabrielle Jackson's view of life. As founder of Fit for the Kingdom Ministries and Chiseled & Curved Fitness, she is a fitness trainer and health coach, who specializes in mind and body wellness, nutrition, and strength training. She's passionate about devoting her efforts to helping others understand the true meaning of fitness. She stresses the importance of creating a well-rounded lifestyle that allows us to excel in life. Gabrielle is currently pursing a Masters Degree at Alabama Agricultural & Mechanical University. Gabrielle strives daily to improve the livelihood of others while offering practical skills to promote overall health and fitness.

Contents

Introduction

Stop. Find a mirror. Quick! Do you see what I see? You are absolutely stunning. What I love even more is what human eyes can not see, and that's your beautiful, healthy spirit. This devotional was designed just for well-rounded, kingdom minded servants of God. People just like you.

I know what you are thinking. How can I know you? I don't know your struggles. I don't know what you've had to endure. You're right. I don't. And I don't have to. Scripture tells me that each of us are fearfully and wonderfully made. Yes, servant of God, that includes you. Marvelous are the works of our God. He has made us in His image, inside and out.

Allow this devotional to serve you as you embark upon your journey to complete wellness – physically, mentally, and spiritually. It was designed to encourage and equip you to live a healthier lifestyle in conjunction to the Word of God.

My prayer is that you learn what it truly means to be *Fit for the Kingdom*. I challenge YOU to commit the next 30 days to your fitness! These devotionals only take two to three minutes to read. That's shorter than the time it takes you to upload the perfect selfie to Instagram! After you read each devotional, journal your thoughts. Writing can be so therapeutic! It's a great way to chart your spiritual growth.

Here's to being truly *Fit for the Kingdom*! What are you waiting for? Turn the page already!

F.I.T.

How F.I.T. are we for the Kingdom of God? God has not only called us to be spiritually fit, but to be well-rounded believers in the body of Christ. Therefore, we haven't been called to be proficient in a *few* things of God, but in *all* things. Ultimately, God desires well-rounded believers who can serve Him through ministering to others. The first step in becoming F.I.T. for God's kingdom is to be intentional about the time we spend with Him. This begins with a healthy prayer life. We must spend Frequent Intentional Time with God to hear what He desires to do through us. It is also through prayer that we gain the strength we need to carry out the purpose He has set for our lives.

Prayer Starter: Dear God, thank You for allowing Your grace and mercy to cover me each day. Now, I ask that You strengthen me for the tasks You have set for my life. May I not grow weary, but lean onto Your unwavering promises.

Scripture Focus: Matthew 6:33 & 3 John 1:2

Journal Topic: What are the tasks in which God has set before you? Do you feel equipped?

Day Two

FREQUENCY

Day upon day we converse with our coworkers, friends, and family, yet neglect God, who is there with us EVEN when we give other things and people more attention than we give Him. Friends and coworkers have the capability of leaving, but we serve an omnipresent God, who is with us always. He desires us to be in constant communication with Him. Evaluate how frequently you are in communication with God. Don't just talk to him when you need him. Often, we view talking to God as an obligation when in actuality, it's a privilege. Yes, He gives us free will, but He expects us to choose Him every time.

Prayer Starter: Father God, thank You for being with me always. Now, I pray that I will begin to grow a deeper relationship with You, that when I pray it's not out of obligation or routine, but because You're worthy and You deserve all the praise, glory, and honor.

Scripture Focus: Daniel 6:10 & 1 Thessalonians 5:16-18

Journal Focus: Daniel prayed to God three times a day because he had a disciplined prayer life. What steps will you take to develop a disciplined prayer life?

Day Three

INTENTIONAL

Just as God was intentional when He formed us in our mother's wombs, strategically planning out each detail of our lives, so should we be intentional about every encounter we have with God. Avoid stagnant routines of praying out of habit. Oftentimes, we fail to be intentional with God because we become so busy spinning our wheels. Cut away unnecessary tasks daily, and schedule fulfilling time with God in prayer. God is calling us out of the land of stagnation and into the kingdom of intent. Today, take some time to meditate on God's intentional plan for your life. We haven't seen nor heard the glorious things He wishes to do for us, and the great works He desires to do through us.

7

Prayer Starter: Dear God, thank You for strategically molding me into the person You have allowed me to become. Now, I ask that You continue to cultivate me, continue to build me, and continue to guide me down Your paths of righteousness.

Scripture Focus: Psalm 139:13-16 & Jeremiah 1:5

Journal Focus: What distracts you from spending intentional time with God?

TIME

When we enter any type of relationship, we're determined to learn that person on a deeper level. Over time, they begin to reveal more and more of themselves, and we reciprocate this action. This is the way our relationship should be with God. We should set aside quality time just for Him. Ask Him questions, and wait for a response. Seek His Godly counsel, and wait for His guidance. The more time we spend in His presence, the more He will begin to reveal Himself and who we are in Him. We live in a world where everyone and everything is competing for our attention, but why should God have to compete with the world He created? Spend some quality time with God today.

Prayer Starter: Father God, thank You for Your presence that rests on me like never before. Now, I ask that You forgive me for placing people and possessions above You. Help me to learn how to put You first and place my trust in Your faithfulness no matter the circumstances.

Scripture Focus: Matthew 6:6, Luke 10:38-42 & Psalm 119:105

Journal Focus: Think about your relationship status with God. How has God revealed Himself to you lately?

UNDERSTANDING MY ROLE

G od is our director, and we're merely characters in His movie. As God goes before us to orchestrate each day, it's important that we understand our roles. In movies, there are usually eight main character roles, the protagonist, antagonist, mentor, tempter, sidekick, skeptic, emotional, and logical. As characters, it's our responsibility to bring God's word to life and allow His righteousness to be shown throughout our lives. Ask God to reveal your role daily. Refer to your script (The Word of God) and stick to your lines! Remember that other characters are watching as well. Today, allow your actions to reflect God's love, will, and purpose for your life.

Prayer Starter: Father God, thank You for the calling You have placed on my life. Now, I ask that You help me to find who I am in You. Help me to define my role in Your kingdom so that my desires reflect Your purpose for my life.

Scripture Focus: Luke 9:57-62 & 2 Timothy 2:15

Journal Focus: How are you bringing God's word to life?

_____

_____

_____

_____

_____

_____

_____

HUNGRY, BUT HUMBLED

As humans, we are created to hunger. God created us that way, both physically and spiritually. As Christians, we must ask ourselves, what are we hungry for? Are we hungrier for the things of this world than we are to be good stewards of what God has blessed us with? Are we hungrier for status than we are to be loyal servants unto God? We often find ourselves out in the world searching for things that only give temporary satisfaction when God offers us 'manna' for lifelong satisfaction. Our level of humbleness is predicated on what we are hungry for. A hunger for this world leaves us unsatisfied every time, whereas a hunger for God guarantees life everlasting.

Prayer Starter: Lord, thank You continuously working on my behalf. Help me to realize that everything I do and everything I'm connected to should bring glory to Your name. Humble me so that I may stand boldly in Your word.

Scripture Focus: Deuteronomy 8:3, Matthew 6:16-18 & 2 Samuel 22:28

Journal Focus: What are you hungry for?

_____

_____

_____

_____

_____

Day Seven

THE POWER OF
SELF-CONTROL

We were bought for a high price. Therefore, our bodies are not our own. Although God gives us free will, His will is that we choose Him above ALL things. God gives us free will because He wants us to exercise self-control. We often think that we're free to do whatever we please, but in an essence we're still captive to our own selfish desires. Think of self-control as a muscle. The more we exercise it, the stronger it becomes. We exercise our self-control through our consistency, discipline, and our willingness to simply say no. Exercise self-control in your life daily through fasting, budgeting, and spending your time doing things that glorify God and strengthen His kingdom.

Prayer Starter: Dear Lord, thank You for your discipline, for I understand that You chastise those You love. Help me to seek Your face in all that I do and turn away from my selfish desires. Transform me now so that our hearts may intertwine.

Scripture Focus: 1 Corinthians 6:19-20, Proverbs 13:3 & 1 Peter 13-16

Journal Focus: How will you choose to exercise self-control today? Will it be through your eating habits, saving money, or learning how to say no?

SPIRITUAL MUSCLES

We live in a society where much emphasis is placed on physical fitness, yet physical fitness means nothing if we're not spiritually fit. What good is it to be fit for the world, yet unfit for the kingdom of God? Our desire to build physical muscles should come second to developing our spiritual muscles. Diseases can infect our physical bodies, but a healthy spiritual body can carry us through any tragedy we face. We must be fully clothed in the armor of God to stand firm against all strategies of the devil. There are certain battles that aren't fought in the physical sense, but in the spiritual realm. We build our spiritual muscles by exercising our unwavering faith in God's promises for our lives.

Prayer Starter: Lord, thank You for the promises You have spoken over my life. Help me to stay steadfast and immovable in Your word, so that I may develop a closer and deeper relationship with You.

Scripture Focus: 1 Timothy 4:7-9 & Ephesians 6:11-12

Journal Focus: What will you do to begin intense spiritual training?

_____

_____

_____

_____

_____

SPIRITUAL PLATEAU

A plateau is a flat, plain area. There are no mountain highs or valley lows. We often encounter seasons in our lives where we hit a spiritual plateau. After God has elevated us to a certain level, we gain a sense of entitlement and get comfortable in mediocrity. As a result, our progress slows, and we become frustrated. We feel as if we're at a standstill, and God has forgotten about us when in actuality, God is showing us that the tactics it took to climb the first hill won't be effective on the next hill. In the physical sense, the higher we climb the thinner the air becomes. In the spiritual realm, the higher we go in God, the more we have to trust the process and the more we must dig deeper into His word. Avoid becoming stagnant and mediocre by constantly seeking God for vision and direction. Be obedient and allow God to elevate you to become all that He desires.

19

Prayer Starter: Lord, I thank You for this season of preparation. Thank You for providing provision for this next season. Now, I ask that You remove the blinders off of my eyes so that I see all the glorious things You desire to do in my life.

Scripture Focus: 1 Corinthians 15:58

Journal Focus: In what areas have you become stagnant and mediocre?

THE BALANCING ACT

The Pharisees were masters of wrapping up their sins respectively. They made themselves appear to work hard and perform good deeds, yet they lacked morals. They would judge and point out the sins of others, but would never evaluate their actions. Many of us are just like the Pharisees. We live two separate lives. We live a life that we allow others to see, and our personal lives look nothing like what we appear to be. It's key that we do self-inventory if we desire to break the strong holds off our lives. We have to be consistent in our actions. Our public lives should be cohesive with our personal lives. God doesn't bless mess; He blesses progress.

Prayer Starter: Lord thank You for remaining consistent despite my inconsistency. Help me to be plugged into You and not things of the world. For I understand that I wasn't truly living until I started living life for You.

Scripture Focus: Luke 5:30-39 & 1 Peter 5:7

Journal Focus: In what areas do you need to practice what you preach?

BE YE TRANSFORMED

Each day God blesses us with a clean slate. We're forgiven of our sins, and we're promised a new set of grace & mercy. Because God continuously washes us clean as snow, it does God an injustice for His children to return to unclean situations. After God has released us from our issues, what good does it serve for us to return to the same situations? The Bible talks specifically about filling old wineskins with new wine. Over time, the old wineskins will burst, causing everything it touches to be tainted. Though we can never thank God enough for all that He does, we can, however, show our appreciation by steering clear of that in which we've been delivered.

Prayer Starter: Father God, help me to completely submit to Your will. Create in me a pure heart that's truly out for the desires of Your heart. Continue to renew my soul each and everyday and create in me a steadfast spirit.

Scripture Focus: Luke 5:37-38 & Psalm 51:10

Journal Focus: Have you submitted completely to God's will in your life?

_____

_____

_____

_____

_____

_____

Day Twelve

CLEAN OUT THE FRIDGE!

Our refrigerators reflect what's on the inside of us. Many of us are guilty of collecting leftovers. We have every intention of eating it, but we allow time to pass. As time passes the food spoils and is no longer consumable. Once the food has spoiled we don't want to deal with it, so we allow it to sit in our refrigerators until it begins to stink up the entire house. This is the way we handle a lot of situations in our lives. We allow negative and painful situations to sit and fester until it changes who we are inside out. At some point, we must clean out the fridge! It's time to get rid of those things that have held us bondage. We have to rid ourselves of things that no longer serve a purpose and fill our lives with connections that help us grow.

Prayer Starter: Father God, thank you for correction in my wrong. I ask now that you replenish me where I am weak. Give me the strength to remove any and everything that's not promoting growth in my life. Now, allow me go forth and complete your assignment for my life.

Scripture Focus: Leviticus 19:6-7

Journal Focus: What "spoiled" situations are you holding on to?

Day Thirteen

PROVISION OF RESTRICTIONS

Submitting our will to God can be scary because we're afraid of the unknown. We struggle with submissiveness because we think we're missing out on life. We think that because we're servants of God we'll be restricted, but that couldn't be further from the truth. The longer we sit at God's feet, the more He'll begin to replace our old desires with His desires, therefore, we lack nothing. We follow the same suite as it pertains to our physical lifestyles. We think that if we can't eat what we desire then we're missing out on life, however, the longer we go without a certain food the less we'll crave and the more we gain. We gain consistency, discipline and self-control – all things that are pleasing to God. We aren't restricted if we are gaining more than what we lost.

Prayer Starter: Lord, I thank You for Your provision. Thank You for showing Yourself mighty and strong in all areas of my life. Help me to change my outlook and develop more discipline in all things of You.

Scripture Focus: 1 Peter 2:9 & Romans 12:2

Journal Focus: Where can you begin to practice more restriction?

BUSY VS. ACTIVE

We live in a world where we glamorize the thought of being busy. We run everywhere and get nowhere; doing everything, yet achieving nothing. We allow ourselves to become so busy in the world that we become inactive in everything God has set forth for us. The Bible teaches us about Mary and Martha. When Jesus came to visit, Martha was so busy with her daily routines that she missed Jesus in her own house. On the other hand, Mary sat at Jesus' feet and actively listened as He taught. Many of us are just like Martha. We're so busy with our daily routines that we miss out on what God is saying and the lessons He desires us to learn. We must be intentional and concerned about everything God has placed before us. Instead of glorifying being busy, let's desire to be active. When we are active in the desires of God, we engage in our true purpose.

Prayer Starter: Lord, I thank You for the assignment You have placed before me. Now, I ask that You train my eyes and ears to be able to see your will and hear Your voice even in the midst of calamity. Allow Your will to be done in each and every area of my life.

Scripture Focus: Luke 11:38-41

Journal Focus: Are you active in the positions God has placed you?

WHOLENESS

God requires wholeness within the body of Christ. The body wouldn't work cohesively if even just one body part were broken or missing. To work efficiently as one body, we first have to ensure that we're whole as a separate entity. The wholeness of the body determines its health and success. Many of us can't operate as a whole because we're too busy masking and suppressing our emotions instead of facing them head on. We have to be more concerned about tending to the body of Christ than we were about finding the next thing to complete us. Before you enter new organizations or relationships, GO TO GOD IN PRAYER! Wait patiently for a response. It's vital that you have a great understanding of who you are as an individual. If not, you will allow that organization or relationship to make you who are, but not who God intended you to be.

Prayer Starter: Dear God, thank You for showing me who I am in You, and who I am not without You. Thank You for helping me to realize that I can't do this on my own, but through You, I can become complete and victorious.

Scripture Focus: James 1:1-8, Philippians 4:6-7 & 1 Corinthians 12:27

Journal Focus: What have you connected to in order to feel complete?

RUN THE RACE

No matter where we are in life, our faith must outweigh our position. God doesn't move because you are experienced or in a high ranking position. God will bless the mailroom worker before the CEO if he has faith in where he's going. God will use unexpected channels to bring glory to His name. If it doesn't bring glory to His name, He's not in it. Now is not the time for us to get discouraged about our position or lack of experience. Now is the time for us to activate our faith and believe God for what He's about to do in our lives. "The race is not given to the swift nor to the strong, but to the one who endures till the end."

Prayer Focus: Lord, I thank You for Your faithfulness. Now, I ask that You cultivate in me a heart of expectancy. I'm expecting for You to do what looks to be impossible, but I know nothing is too impossible for my God.

Scripture Focus: Ecclesiastes 9:11, Matthew 17:20, & 1Samuel 7-14, Hebrews 12:1-2

Journal Focus: Where do you desire elevation?

RESTORATION

We often question our life's events. We wonder why God has allowed certain things to happen. He's allowed us to experience mistrust, pain, and hurt. He's allowed relationships to end. He allowed us to lose our "dream" jobs. God allows the destruction of certain things in our lives because they weren't beneficial to where He desired to take us. God knew that if the decision were left up to us, we would still be holding on to dead situations. As a result, what we thought would be our downfall has become our elevation. God specializes in using broken pieces to rebuild what appeared to be destroyed temples. Be thankful for the tearing down. Be thankful for the breaking. Be thankful that God stepped in when He did. Be thankful that He saw something greater in us than we saw in ourselves.

Prayer Starter: Dear God, thank You for loving me unconditionally. Thank You for blocking everything that served as a hindrance from me gaining a closer relationship with You. Now, I ask that You continue to protect and strengthen me day by day.

Scripture Focus: Jeremiah 32:36-41

Journal Focus: Write about a situation in which you are grateful for God's intervening favor.

Day Eighteen

SECOND WIND

Are you sabotaging your long run by running at the wrong pace and in the wrong direction? We've been serving, sacrificing, and sowing, but are we doing these things at a magnitude that catches God's attention? When we run at the right pace and in the right direction God disperses a second wind. Not because we're perfect, but because we desire to possess the perfection of Christ.

Stay on the course. God is about to reveal and refill! Brace yourself for elevation.

Prayer Starter: Father God, I thank You for this season of elevation. Now, I ask that the higher you take me, the humbler you make me.

Scripture Focus: Philippians 3:12-15 Isaiah 43:18

Journal Focus: Evaluate areas in your life where you need God to breathe a second wind. Are these areas on God's course for your life?

OPEN MOUTHS GET FED

God knows the specifics of our hearts. He knows what we need even before we ask Him. God keeps us in situations for two specific reasons. 1) We haven't learned our lesson and 2) There are something's God won't release simply because we haven't opened our mouths. Some of us are starving because we haven't opened our mouths to receive what God is trying to deposit in our lives. A consistent prayer life doesn't equate to a stress-free life. We can pray 30 times a day, but if our prayers aren't changing things in our lives, we have to reevaluate. Some of us are still praying the prayers we've been taught or the prayers we heard someone else pray. Dig deeper into God's word and learn the true meaning of prayer. God is looking for believers with a new prayer, a new anointing, and a renewed spirit.

Prayer Starter: Father God, thank You for caring so much about me that You are willing to meet every one of my needs. I ask that You continue to mold me, strip me, and build me to be more like You.

Scripture Focus: Matthew 6:6-8, James 1:5

Journal Focus: What do you need? Have you prayed to God about it?

SUPERSET YOUR FAITH

Supersets are great for losing fat and building muscle. They are time efficient and increase muscle activation. This all sounds great, right? You lose weight, save time, and build muscle all at the same time! But, to perform a superset correctly, it requires that you perform two exercises back to back with NO REST in between. So, in an essence, it promises great results, but work must be reinforced to reap the benefits. When we have true faith, it transforms our actions as well as our thoughts. If our lives are remaining the same, it's because we don't truly believe what we claim can be achieved. Our faith and work ethic work together simultaneously. We have to superset our faith and work ethic to the point that neither can fully operate without the other.

Prayer Focus: Father God, thank you for moving so heavily throughout my life that my faith in you is seamless. Thank you for giving me your work ethic of being a God that's worked, working, and will continue to work.

Scripture Focus: James 3:14-16, Proverbs 13:4, Proverbs 14:23 & Proverbs 20:4

Journal Focus: How will you begin to work your faith?

Day Twenty-One

WEIGH-IN(SELF CHECK)

Have you ever caught yourself thinking the worst of a situation before it's even begins? Sometimes, we talk ourselves out of the very thing we know God has told us to do. We begin saying things like, "This is too difficult." "My friends and family will think I'm crazy." "I'm really not qualified for this position." and my personal favorite, "This is taking too long." Meanwhile, God is saying, "No, you may not be certified on paper, but I qualified you long ago! Don't worry about what people say. My opinion is the only one that matters." When we begin to have those thoughts of inadequacy recognize that it's a tactic of the enemy. He desires you to be held captive of your thoughts. Secondly, change your perspective. Instead of pointing out the negatives, find the positives aspects in all situations. Declare war against all forms of negativity. Think positive and show the enemy no mercy!

Prayer Starter: Father God, I thank you for the renewing of my mind. I come against all forms of negativity that try to hinder me from moving forward. I'm declaring victory and denying defeat over every situation that comes my way.

Scripture Focus: Proverbs 15:30 & 1 Peter 5:7

Journal Focus: What are you claiming victory over?

_____

_____

_____

_____

_____

_____

Day Twenty-Two

WEIGHT MANAGEMENT

We often take on more than we should. We take on extra hours at work, spend money on unnecessary items, over-invest ourselves into people or situations and find ourselves carrying weight that God never intended us to carry. It begins to feel as if we've tied a 50-pound weight around our necks. We become comfortable operating in dysfunction. We drag around, hoping no one notices that we've mismanaged our lives and our time with God. The awesome thing about God is that He wishes to remove the unnecessary weight. It's nearly impossible for Him to remove it if we can't first acknowledge that it's causing a problem. Acknowledge that you have taken on too much. Sure, it's hard to drop things we've committed to, but the sooner we drop our own commitments, the sooner we can take on the tasks that God has ordained us to carry.

45

Prayer Starter: Father God, I thank you for allowing me to see my faults and correct my wrongs. Now I ask that you give me the strength to remove things that aren't beneficial to where you desire to elevate me.

Scripture Focus: (2 Corinthians 10: 4-5)

Journal Focus: Evaluate your weight. What excess weight is preventing you from fully experiencing God's glory in your life?

IT HURTS TO STRETCH

Stretching helps break the cycle of soreness. If you're expecting to see a change, stretching is necessary. Stretching helps to prepare you for the workout and helps you to cope with the soreness after the workout. When we decide to make a change in our lifestyles, our bodies fight us every step of the way. It naturally desires to remain comfortable. After a workout we're fatigued, we experience a lack of motivation, and more than anything, our muscles are sore and it hurts for us to stretch. When God stretches us it doesn't feel good, but it is necessary for the growth we desire to see in our lives. The war is with our flesh. Deny your flesh the pleasure of being comfortable. Allow God to stretch you to your capacity. He knows just how far we can go! During the stretching, we realize that we are a lot more flexible than we ever thought we were.

Prayer Starter: Father God, I thank you for my level of flexibility. Now I ask that you strengthen me and help me to be still, for I know that you will fight my battles for me.

Scripture Focus: Ephesians 6:12 & Philippians 4:6-7

Journal Focus: What areas of your life could use a bit more stretching?

A TRAINED EYE

A 'good' eye is an eye that's fixed on God. A good eye is an eye that resolves to see the good in every situation. Sometimes, we allow distractions to detour our focus. We find ourselves so fixated on what's happening in the present that we negate the promises that God has already declared over our lives. Envision your eyes as lamps that provide light for your body. How you decide to view the world is an indication of how much of God's light dwells within you. God desires us to have His spiritual eyesight for guidance, structure, and contentment in all situations. God wants to accomplish mighty things through us. Just as we train our bodies we have to also train our eyesight to be able to see God moving in all areas of our lives. The more we seek, the better our eyesight becomes.

Prayer Starter: Dear God, I thank You for removing the scales off of my eyes. Now, I pray that I'm able to keep my eyes fixed on You. Help me to stay faithful in You, because You have never failed me, and never will.

Scripture Focus: Matthew 6:22, Proverbs 3:5-6 & Psalm 121:1-2

Journal Focus: What are some areas you need God's guiding light?

_____

_____

_____

_____

_____

_____

CONVIENENCE

Convenience has its place, however, it shouldn't play a huge role in our lives. We often do things that are easier just because it's convenient. It's easy to do things that are fitting to our needs, plans, and comfort. What's convenient doesn't always serve us best. It's more convenient to eat out than it is to cook at home, but that doesn't mean it's better for you. Stepping outside of our own flow and into God's plan is sometimes inconvenient, but it is best. When we're placed in uncertain situations God steps in and allows for His light to shine. Unknowingly, God has had us behind the scenes preparing us for this very moment. Now is our time to rise to the occasion and showcase our resiliency! We're going to be able to go places, meet people, and change lives, not because we have the education, skills, or knowledge, but because we're connected to the one who knows ALL.

Prayer Starter: Dear God, thank you for seeing greater in me than I see in myself. Help me to cultivate the mind, heart, and spirit of Christ, so that when people see me, they see you.

Scripture Focus: Joshua 1:9, 1 John 6:4 & 2 Timothy 1:7

Journal Focus: Where is your plan stifling the move of God?

_____

_____

_____

_____

_____

_____

Day Twenty - Six

THE PROCESS OF GROWTH

Sometimes we have to remind ourselves that it's all part of the process. No one enters into a situation having all the answers. It takes grooming, life experience, and growth. In order to **GROW** it requires that we seek **G**odly **R**everence **O**n **W**isdom. We are the branches of God's grapevine. We have to reverence Him in all our ways to receive the nutrients we need to bear the RIGHT fruit. He's currently taking us through the process of cutting and pruning. He's cutting off our branches of fear, hatred, insecurity, and hurt, so that they are to never to return. He's pruning our branches of love, wisdom, stability, forgiveness and confidence so that we can increase in those areas. We're not growing only for ourselves, but to also help others bear the same fruit. In order to be fruitful we have to remain in God, and Him in us.

Prayer Starter: Father God, I thank you for this season of growth. I thank you for this season of cutting and pruning. Although, I may not understand it all, I know that it's all for my greater good. I pray that the more I seek your face, the more wisdom you begin to shower upon me.

Scripture Focus: John 15:1-8

Journal Focus: What are some areas in your life that require a little pruning?

Day Twenty-Seven

TEAMWORK

We often say use the phrase, "There's no I in team," but have we truly embraced its meaning? It literally means, it takes a team to get things accomplished. God doesn't give us mundane aspirations. He gives us dreams to accomplish things that are far bigger than us, far bigger than anything we could have ever imagined for ourselves. He allows us to dream big because he wants us to collaborate with our brothers and sisters in Christ. Nehemiah built a team of people to help him accomplish the goal of rebuilding the wall. God doesn't give us ideas for us to keep to ourselves. He blesses us so that we can be a blessing to others. Because God is so faithful he will begin to strategically align the right people in our paths. We will no longer have to look for people to support us; they will come looking to be supportive.

Prayer Starter: Father God, I thank You for Your provision. Thank You for sending brothers and sisters who are going to be supportive of your vision. Now, I ask that You help me to get out of my own way and allow You to direct my paths.

Scripture Focus: Nehemiah 3 & Ecclesiastes 4:9-12

Journal Focus: Here are a few characteristics of a good team. Evaluate the teams you are a part of. Are these teams effective? How can you help them become more effective?

Characteristics of an effective team:

- Commitment to the team's vision and purpose

- Clear performance goals of what the team wishes to accomplish

- Diversity of skills and personalities

- Effective communication & collaboration

- Strong sense of trust among members

STABILITY IN BALLS

I f you think about the shape of a stability ball, it's round, it has no flat surfaces, it can be bounced, thrown, and rolled; therefore, it has the capability of going wherever the wind blows it. On the other hand, stability balls also build strength, coordination, and increase performance and balance.

Sometimes we can become so dependent on the support of others things, that we fail to realize that God has given us the ability to create our own balance. We find our balance by holding Christ at the center of our being. Lately, have you felt unbalanced or unfocused? Re-center and refocus by honing in on the will of God for your life.

Prayer Focus: Father God, I thank You for laying a solid foundation. Thank You for providing stability when I felt like I had none. Now I ask that You continue to keep me grounded and keep my eyes focused on You.

Scripture Focus: Isaiah 33:6 & James 1:6

Journal Focus: What areas of your life require you to refocus?

_____

_____

_____

_____

_____

Day Twenty-Nine

IT'S OKAY TO BREATHE

Take a deep breath – Hold it – Now Exhale....
Take another deep breath – Hold it – Now
Exhale....

Last one, take a deep breath – Hold it – Now
Exhale....

In the same way we breathe, God requires that we take rest in Him. We take in everything God has deposited into our lives until it's time to release it into the atmosphere. That's just a portion of what ministering God's word is all about. Even in serving, God understands that in order for us to work efficiently, we must take periodic rest to refuel, refocus, and renew.

Take rest in him. Bask in all of God's glory. Allow Him to take your heavy burdens. Seek his face for fresh revelations for your life. Ask Him to give you a fresh word, a fresh prayer, and a refreshed anointing.

Prayer Starter: Father God, thank You for being a resting place in my times of weariness. Continue to strengthen me for it's in You that I find my strength and will to go on.

Scripture Focus: Mark 6:30-32

Journal Focus: Meditate on your life. Take a moment today and rest in God. Schedule in periodic breaks on your calendar.

THE GIFT OF GIVING

G od has given each of us spiritual gifts. I like to think of it as the gift that keeps on giving. God blesses us with gifts, and it's our duty to bless others. Sometimes we develop a self-serving mentality. We begin to think that our gifts belong to us for us. We become possessive, and no one can touch it, see it, or even be a witness to it. What's the point of receiving the gift if you're not willing to share the gift? Before we expose our gifts to others we have to ensure that what's on the inside is not broken or tarnished. When spiritual gifts are exercised properly, they contribute to the overall health and growth of the kingdom of God.

Now I ask, what on earth are you doing for heaven's sake?

Prayer Starter: Father God, I praise You because I am fearfully and wonderfully made. I pray that when people see me, they see You first. Now I ask that You help me to cultivate my spiritual gifts so that I can be a blessing to others.

Scripture Focus: 1 Peter: 4:10-11, Ephesians 4:12 & Ephesians 4:16

Journal Focus: What are your spiritual gifts? How do you share your gift with others?

Gabrielle wants to hear from you! Connect with her today!

Gabrielle Jackson

Email: chiseled.curvedfitness@gmail.com

Website: www.chiseledandcurvedfitness.com

Instagram: @chiseled_curves

Facebook: Gabrielle Jackson

Be sure to leave your book reviews for Fit For the Kingdom at www.amazon.com.

Made in the USA
Lexington, KY
10 March 2017